Right Hand Technique for Guitar

Volume One

with
Audio examples downloadable
from the internet

by
Bruce Arnold

Muse Eek Publishing Company
New York, New York

Copyright © 2001 by Muse Eek Publishing Company. All rights reserved

ISBN 1-890944-54-8

No part of this publication may be reproduced, stored in a
retrieval system, or transmitted, in any form or by any means,
electronic, mechanical, photocopying, recording, or otherwise,
without the prior written permission of the publisher.

Printed in the United States

This publication can be purchased from your local bookstore or by contacting:
Muse Eek Publishing Company
P.O. Box 509
New York, NY 10276, USA
Phone: 212-473-7030
Fax: 212-473-4601
http://www.muse-eek.com
sales@muse-eek.com

Table Of Contents

Acknowledgements   *iii*
About the Author   *iv*
Foreword   *v*
Right Hand Technique   1
Exercise 1   16
Exercise 2   21
Exercise 3   26
Exercise 4   31
Exercise 5   36
Exercise 6   41
Exercise 7   46
Exercise 8   51
Exercise 9   56
Exercise 10   61
Exercise 11   66
Exercise 12   71
Exercise 13   76
Exercise 14   81
Exercise 15   86
Exercise 16   91
Exercise 17   96
Exercise 18   101
Exercise 19   106
Exercise 20   111
Exercise 21   116
Exercise 22   121
Exercise 23   126
Exercise 24   131

Acknowledgments

The author would like to thank Michal Shapiro for her patience and help in proof reading and helpful suggestions.

About the Author

Bruce Arnold is from Sioux Falls, South Dakota. His educational background started with 3 years of music study at the University of South Dakota; he then attended the Berklee College of Music where he received a Bachelor of Music degree in composition. During that time he also studied privately with Jerry Bergonzi and Charlie Banacos.

Mr. Arnold has taught at some of the most prestigious music schools in America, including the New England Conservatory of Music, Dartmouth College, Berklee College of Music, Princeton University and New York University. He is a performer, composer, jazz clinician and has an extensive private instruction practice.

Currently Mr. Arnold is performing with his own "The Bruce Arnold Trio," and "Eye Contact" with Harvie Swartz, as well as with two experimental bands, "Release the Hounds" a free improv group, and "Spooky Actions" which re-interprets the work of 20th Century classical masters.

His debut CD "Blue Eleven" (MMC 2036J) received great critical acclaim, and his most recent CD "A Few Dozen" was released in January 2000. The Los Angeles Times said of this release "Mr. Arnold deserves credit for his effort to expand the jazz palette."

For more information about Mr. Arnold check his website at http://www.arnoldjazz.com This website contains audio examples of Mr. Arnold's compositions and a workshop section with free downloadable music exercises.

Foreword

Through my years of teaching I have come across many students who have developed right hand problems because of improper technique. Their problems ranged from slow and inaccurate execution to tendonitis. Some of these students had quit completely because of pain before they came to me. This book covers the techniques I use to help students get a strong and healthy right hand that they can use it for a life time of playing. It is important to mention that if you are picking this book up for the first time because you have severely injured yourself by repetitive movement, you must work into to this book **very slowly** and **never play through pain.**

Although I have provided you with many exercises to help develop your right hand technique it is important that you apply this method to your own style of playing. Use common sense when practicing the exercises. Always start slowly, watch yourself in a mirror to make sure you are using the correct movement, then finally, apply your new technique to your own musical ideas.

There are 24 exercises presented in the back of this book. Each exercise is accompanied by an audio example. These audio examples can be downloaded for free from the internet at http://www.muse-eek.com. The audio files use midifiles which can be played on a Mac or IBM computer by using a midifileplayer or any sequencer program. Midifile players are available for free at many sites on the internet. muse-eek.com lists a few places to download this software.

Muse Eek Publishing has created a website with a FAQ forum for all my books. If you have any questions about anything contained in this book feel free to contact me at FAQ@muse-eek.com and I will happy to post an answer to your question. My goal is to educate and help you reach a higher degree of musical ability.

Bruce Arnold
New York, New York

Right Hand Technique

Right hand technique on guitar is one of the most misunderstood and overlooked aspects of guitar playing. With the myriad of right hand styles used by guitarists it is difficult to know which technique is best. Whether you are an occasional strummer of the guitar or are seeking to become a "world class" guitarist, utilizing the muscles of your right arm in the proper way will insure you years of pain-free development.

Volume 1 of this series will cover the basics for good right hand technique. It is a big commitment to stop one's current right hand technique and start on a new course, but I have found that the students I teach have substantially better speed and accuracy in 6 to 8 months utilizing the suggestions found in this book. These students usually come to me experiencing pain from improper technique. Even partial implementation of the methods put forth in this book will help you to play more fluidly.

The guitar is a very versatile instrument and is capable of many different sounds and styles, and the right hand is your tool for creating many of them. Volume one of the right hand technique series will only cover some of the more basic techniques. Styles such as harmonics, muting, alternative picking applications etc. will be covered in future volumes.

Frequently when people discuss right hand technique they overlook the most basic things. Guitar placement in relation to your body and pick placement within your hand have to be addressed before proper right-hand movement can be obtained. These two aspects along with the correct movement of your forearm and elbow comprise a right hand technique that can be sustained for a lifetime.

It is important to remember that every person is built differently. What works for one person may cause severe pain to another. Don't figure that because your friend or superstar hero plays with the guitar at knee level means that it will work for you. If you are experiencing pain or if you have tried a technique and don't feel that you are progressing, start questioning the wisdom of continuing with a position that's probably not right for you. Admittedly, the method presented here is tedious and time consuming but keep in mind that it will not cause you a fraction of the anguish you will experience if you have to start a new way of picking half way through your career, or never reach your goal because of bad form.

GUITAR PLACEMENT

The placement of the guitar in relation to your body is a tricky subject because of the many body types that exist. (This applies to both people _and_ guitars!) Long and short arms and torso, body weight and size can mean further adjustments have be made to the basic suggestions that follow.

You should always stand up while practicing any of the exercises in this book. After you have mastered these techniques you will know the proper position to use when sitting.

In general the guitar should be slightly above the hip region. If the guitar is placed too low it will adversely effect your left hand position. The wrist of the left hand will be too bent to play quickly and without pain. **The wrists and elbows of both arms should be in the middle of their radius to avoid injury**.

If the guitar is too high, you will have a tendency to raise or hold up your shoulders. This "shrugging" will end up causing you pain in both upper arms and shoulder regions, as well as in the neck and back. To check if you have the proper position for the guitar, strap on the guitar and allow your right arm to fall free at your side. Raise your arm from the elbow while swinging your arm over the guitar into a position where your hand is halfway between the highest fret on the guitar and the bridge where the strings rest. Try not to let your pick fall directly above a pickup if possible; the pickup will amplify the sound of the pick striking the strings.

Make sure you are not raising your right arm from the shoulder to place your hand in the proper place above the strings. Also check to make sure your left hand doesn't have to make a sharp bend to access the notes around the 3rd fret low E string. (Sometimes a change must be made in left hand technique to get your wrist not to bend more than 20° or 30° when playing down in 1st to 3rd position on the guitar). Make sure you aren't lifting from your left shoulder to play any notes on the fretboard.

It also should be mentioned that sometimes the strap screws have to be moved on certain types of guitars in order for your hand and arm to lie across the instrument comfortably.

PICK PLACEMENT

The most natural placement of the pick is having the thumb on one side and the index (1st) and middle finger (2nd) supporting the other side. If you play with a style in which you need access to your 2nd, 3rd and 4th finger to pluck strings, place the pick between the index finger and the thumb. **You should never squeeze too tightly when holding the pick.** You will notice pain from the thumb all the way to the elbow developing over time if you continually squeeze too hard. The pick should be held only firmly enough to keep it from falling out of your fingers when you play. Many guitarist feel they need to hold the pick very firmly especially when really bearing down on the string for heavy accents. It is much better to use your forearm (area between your wrist and elbow) to access the energy needed for these types of attacks. The forearm muscle has the bulk to put up with this kind of stress.

In general the pick should barely touch the top of the strings. The more you dig into the strings the slower you will play and the more energy you will need. By keeping your pick skating across the top of each string you can quickly move from string to string without having to raise your pick to move to the next string. **Economy of motion is the key to fast, accurate, and pain free playing.**

RIGHT HAND FINGER PLACEMENT

While the pick is being held by the thumb and 1st, or thumb and 1st and 2nd fingers, the other fingers should remain relaxed. Once again allow your hand to fall to your side. Notice your fingers usually form a slight arc. This is the same way your fingers should look when you bring your hand around to play. You certainly should not be using any fingers as anchor points and your fingers should not be folded into your palm. Any excess tension in your fingers will translate into pain in your forearm sooner or later. If your fingers feel like they are getting in the way of the strings when you try to pick, pull the pick out so there is less of it in between your fingers, and this will help in the adjustment. It should also be mentioned that you shouldn't be resting the palm of your hand on the bridge. This is a common problem I see in guitarists; by resting their palm on the bridge they create a situation where all movement has to come from the wrist or thumb.

THE ELBOW AS THE PIVOT POINT

The movement from string to string should come from the elbow, not the wrist. If the wrist is used to move from string to string you will end up with a severe turn in the wrist by the time you reach the high E string, and this will eventually cause pain. **You should not initiate any movement from the wrist.** To practice this, start by strumming all the strings from the low E string to the high E string.

Initiate the movement from your elbow and make sure your wrist is straight and in the middle of its radius. Start with only down strokes. Let your hand feel as if gravity is pulling it down, not as if you are using your muscles to move the pick across the strings. Use wide strokes. Start well before the string, and continue past the high E string. (If you are attempting this after having previously injured your arm from playing, start with a few repetitions and space it out throughout a day.) You should continue this until you feel as if you have control and **always stop if you experience any pain.** After mastering the down stroke start strumming using both up and down strokes. Again, use wide strokes, and remember to let gravity pull your arm down on the down strokes and initiate all movement from the elbow. When this begins to feel comfortable you should start to limit your range of motion so that you only strum the distance between the two E strings with no wasted motion. This will take time to master but is an important step on the way to proper technique.

When you feel as if you have this under control you want to start picking each string using only your elbow as the initiator of the movement. There are many exercises you can do once you have reached this point. I would first concentrate on picking each string until you have developed an economy of motion; i.e. you are not hitting other strings and you feel as if you can maintain control from your elbow. Make sure that the fingers not holding the pick are loose and relaxed. If you feel pain or tightness in any finger or up into the forearm this is usually caused by a tightening of the fingers. Also remember not to hold the pick too tightly as this will also cause you problems.

Using the elbow to pick each string is just an interim method to develop control. Do not attempt to play quickly using this method unless you are doing "across the strings" sweeps.

It should be mentioned at this point that the right hand is the main instigator of rhythm for a guitarist. If you have been using another method of picking before this, you really have to retrain your mind to send the "rhythm signals" to new muscles. This will take time to develop. I have found a method that will greatly accelerate your mind's ability to readjust these "rhythm signals". Rhythm studies are the best to begin with, because they don't require you to use the left hand. Make sure to master each exercise before moving on.

ONE PICK PER STRING

Start by picking each string with one down stroke and then move to the next string. Start on the low E and work your way up to the high E string and back down. Play all the notes as eighth notes. **Do not play this fast;** it is just a first step in learning a new technique.

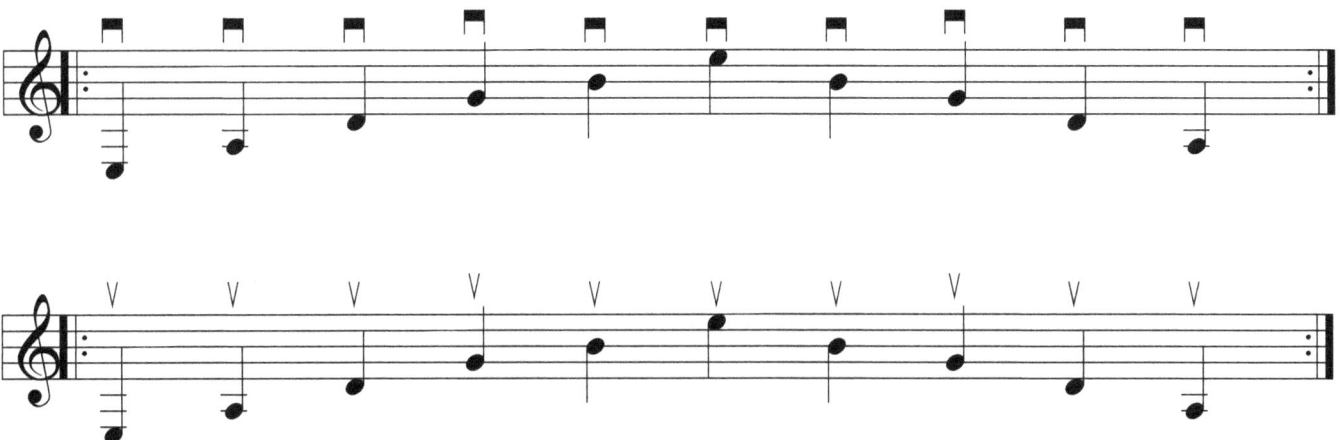

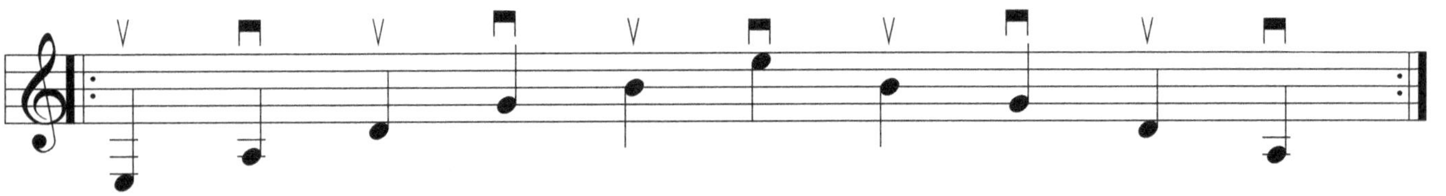

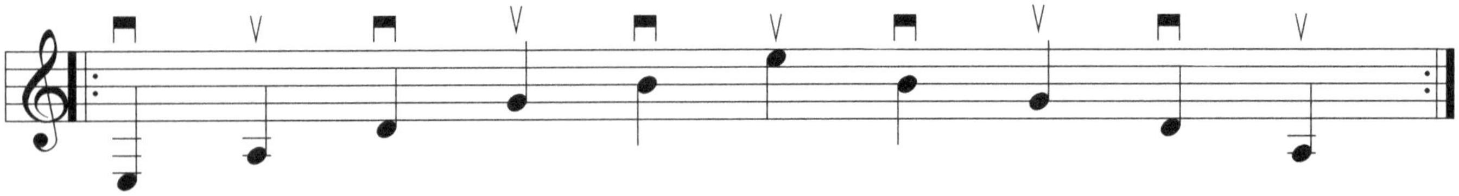

Try using the different picking combinations presented with exercises 1, 2, 5, 7, 9, 10, 13, 17, 19, and 22 in the back of this book.

TWO PICKS PER STRING

Start by picking each string with two down strokes and then move to the next string. Start on the low E and work your way up to the high E string and back down. Play all the notes as eighth notes. Again, do not attempt to play this fast as it is just a first step in learning a new technique.

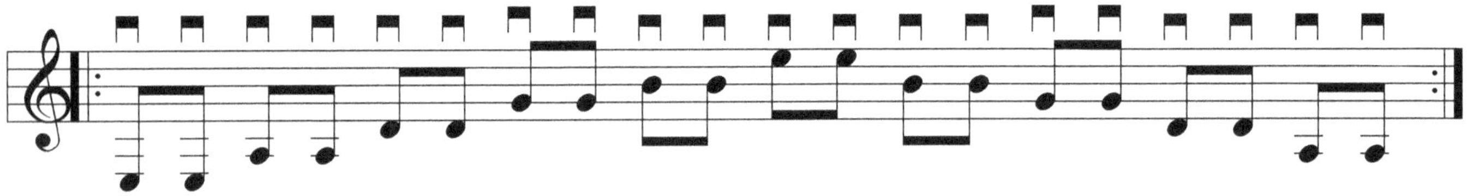

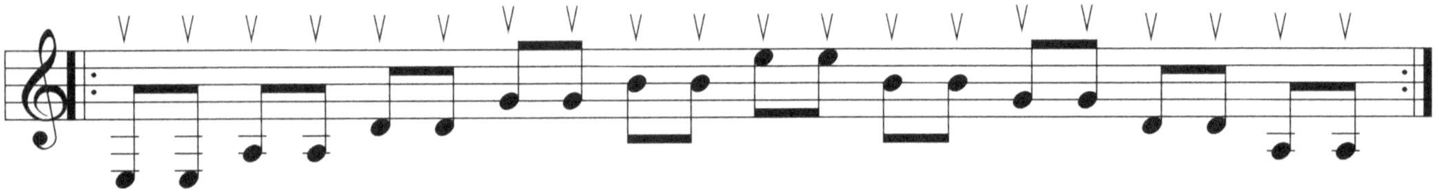

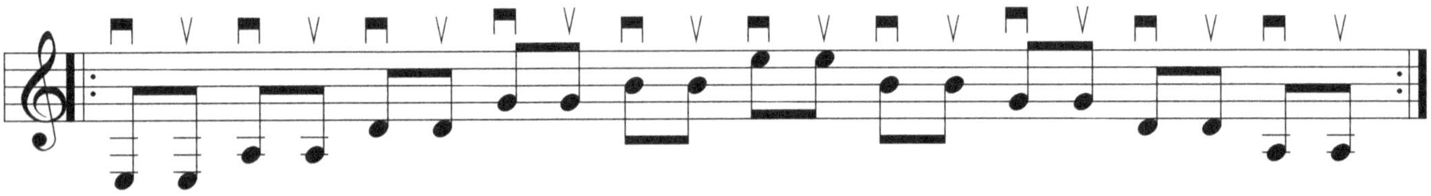

Also try applying the different picking patterns presented here to exercise 14 on page 81..

3 PICKS PER STRING

Picking three times on each string has more combinations. Remember you are not playing these examples for speed, but for **control**. Play these examples as triplets, eighths or sixteenths.

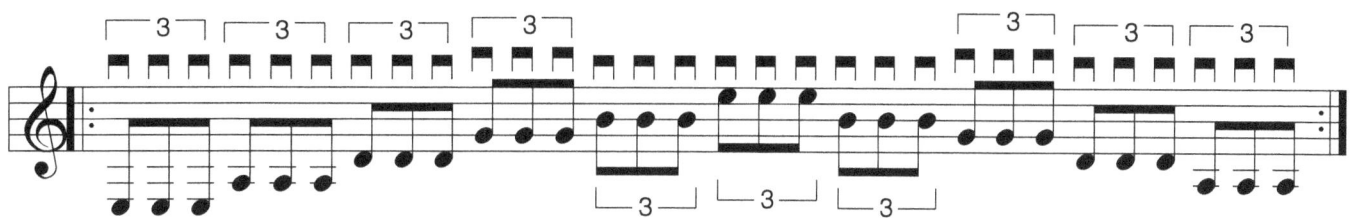

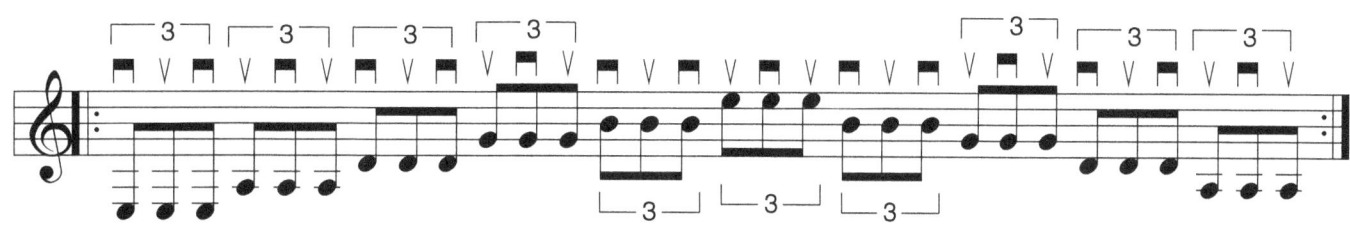

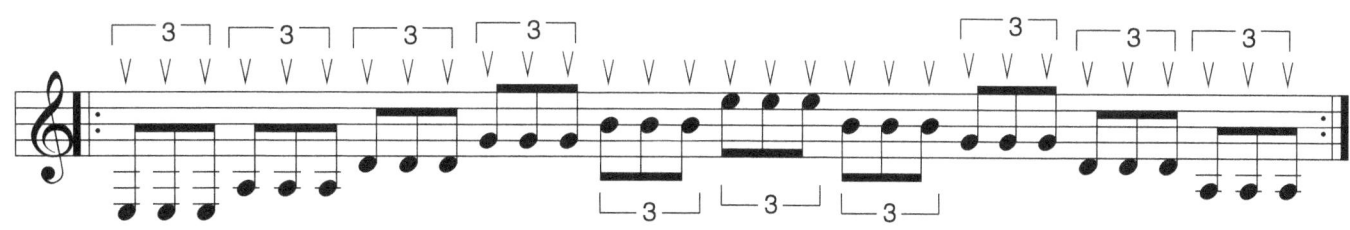

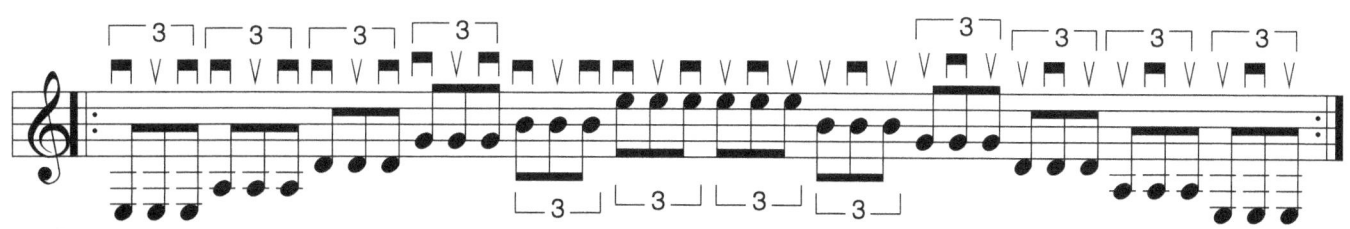

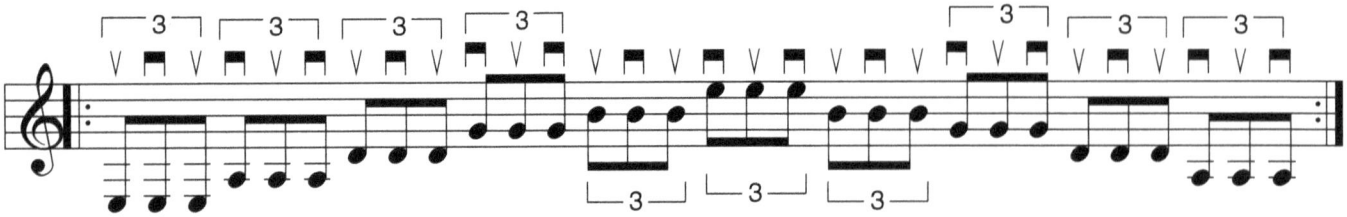

You also can work on exercise 3 and 16 in the back of this book to help develop this technique. Also try applying the different picking patterns to these exercises.

FOUR NOTES PER STRING

Pick each string four times then move to the next string. You can also work on the example 4 and 15 found in the back of this book. Try using both picking patterns with these exercises.

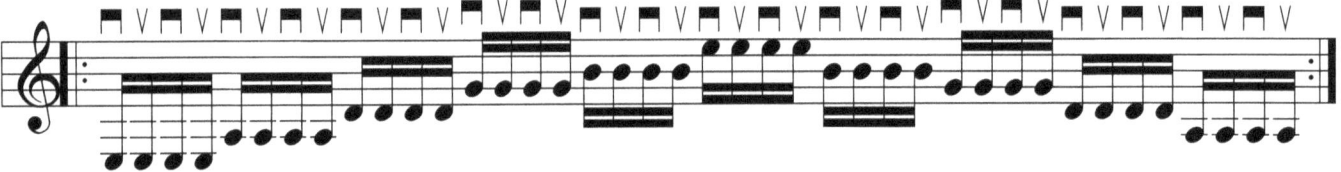

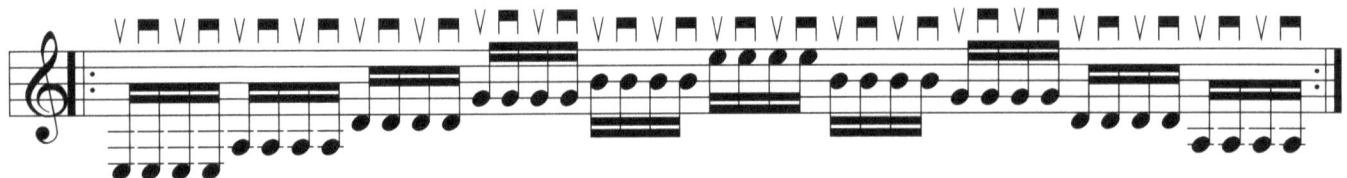

STRUMMING

While developing the aforementioned patterns you can also start on common strumming patterns. In the examples below the ⊓ is used to designate a down strum and the V is used to designate an up strum. Try these strumming patterns at different speeds to develop dexterity. Remember that all movement should come from the elbow. Make sure your wrist is straight and you are holding the pick only as hard as you need to, and that your other fingers are relaxed

STRUMMING PATTERNS CONTINUED

SWEEP AND CROSS STRING PICKING

Sweep picking and cross string picking are closely related to strumming. For instance, when you sweep across all six strings, it shouldn't feel as if you are picking each string individually, but are just letting the pick strum across the strings in a single movement. If you want to develop your sweep picking and cross string picking I have supplied you with rhythm examples in the back of this book to develop that technique. Audio examples of these exercises can be downloaded at www.arnoldjazz.com/workshop. The sky is the limit on how fast you want to play these exercises. With a relaxed hand and forearm you should quickly notice improvement. I recommend using examples 1, 2, 5, 6, 7, 8, 9. 10, 11, 12, 13, 18, 19, 20, 21, 22, 23, and 24 a supplement exercises for developing sweep picking and cross string technique. Remember to play these sweep and cross string picking patterns by moving only your elbow.

SWEEP PATTERNS CONTINUED

THE FOREARM AS A PIVOT POINT

You will find a plethora of different methods that guitarists use to pick each string. It is common to see the thumb, wrist, or elbow used to initiate movement. But the muscles in the thumb and upper arm are not able to keep up with the demands placed on them when trying to access more demanding techniques, and while the elbow can be used for strumming and sweep picking, is too big a muscle to control for complex picking patterns unless you really tense up your arm. Tension inevitably leads to trouble - from slow and inaccurate technique to tendonitis or carpal tunnel syndrome. Only the forearm (the area between the wrist and elbow) has a muscle big enough and subtle enough to supply the endurance and precision needed. Therefore the movement of the pick should come from your forearm. This forearm movement is the same movement used to drink a glass of water, turn a screw driver or open a door. Another way to experience this movement is to lay your arm flat on a table and lift your thumb up using your forearm. Don't use the muscle in your thumb but allow your forearm to pick your thumb up off the table.

When you start applying this movement to picking, you will find it extremely awkward at first. Have patience. Usually within a few weeks you will feel a light, pain-free control taking over that will allow you infinite development.

Start this new movement without the guitar. Place your arm across your upper stomach area with your pick in your hand. Move your forearm muscle which will move your wrist and in turn move the pick back and forth. Start with large movements so you get the feeling of using the forearm. With time you will want to limit the range of motion until it feels like your arm is shimmering with a very small movement. (This can be practiced anywhere without the guitar.) When you feel comfortable try this with your guitar on. Try to pick a string using alternate picking. Don't worry about picking more than one string, your control will develop over time. When you feel that you can accurately picked each string with a down and up stroke you can slowly start to limit the range of motion of your pick. Limiting your range of movement will require more control over your forearm muscle so give yourself at least a couple of weeks before you expect to see results. (Remember not to tense up any part of your arm as you start to limit the range of motion) As you feel you are gaining more control start working again using the exercises found on the next couple of pages. When these feel comfortable you can use exercises 1, 2, 5, 7, 9, 10, 13, 17, 19, and 22 in the back of the book. Once again, audio examples of these exercises can be downloaded at www.arnoldjazz.com/workshop. You also can use the "Rhythms Volume One and Two" at slow tempos to gain more control and begin to teach your forearm all the different rhythm combinations.

ONE PICK PER STRING

Start by picking each string with one down stroke and then move to the next string. Start on the low E and work your way up to the high E string and back down. Your elbow will be used to moving your hand from the low E string to the high E string while forearm movement will be the instigator of the pick attack. At first use wide strokes to get the feeling of using your forearm. As time goes on, make this movement smaller to develop more speed and accuracy.

All these exercises should be practiced slowly at first. As you improve try to limit the motion of your pick, so you move as little as possible

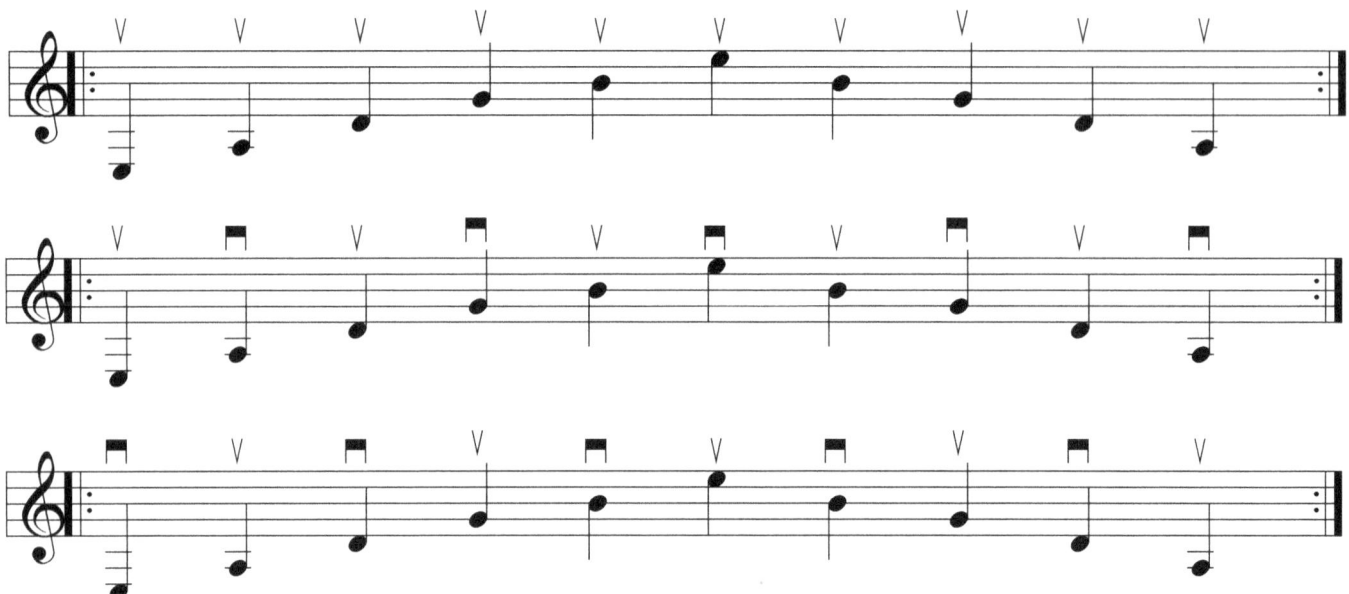

Try using the different picking combinations presented with exercises 1, 2, 5, 7, 9, 10, 13, 17, 19, and 22 in the back of this book.

TWO PICKS PER STRING

Start by picking each string with two down strokes and then move to the next string. These two note exercises will prepare you for playing pentatonic scales or any other melodic pattern where there are two notes on each string. Again, as you improve try to apply economy of motion to gain speed. You can also work on exercise 14 on page 81. Also try applying the different picking patterns presented here to exercise 14.

3 PICKS PER STRING

Picking three times on each string will prepare you for most scales. **Remember, at first you are not playing these examples for speed but for control.** Use your elbow to move your pick from the low E string to the high E string, and your forearm to pick each string. If you feel tension in your forearm check your little finger and ring finger to make sure they are relaxed. Speed will come as you limit your range of motion. You also can work on exercise 3 and 16 to help develop this technique. Try applying the different picking patterns to these exercises.

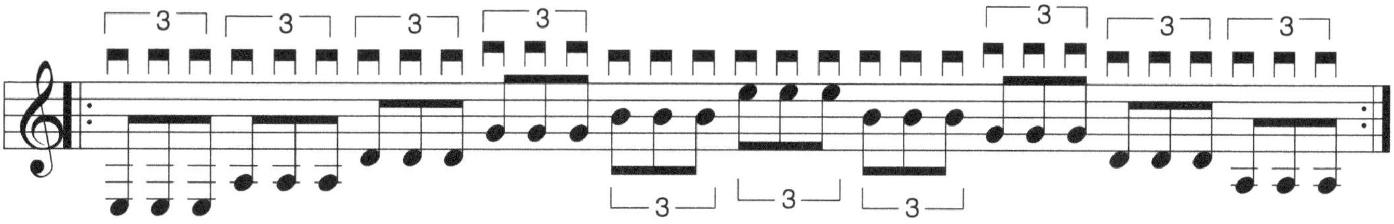

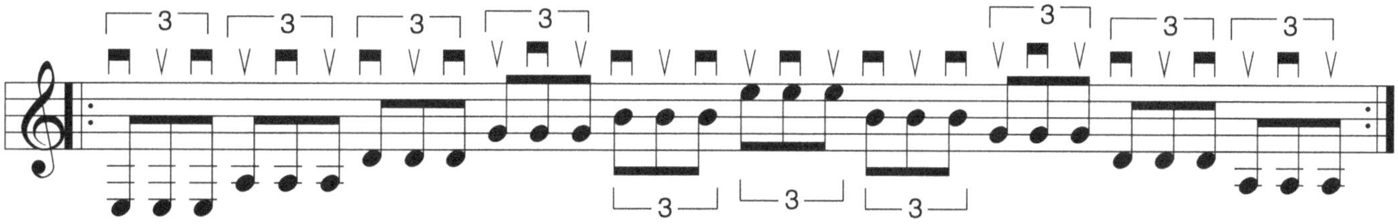

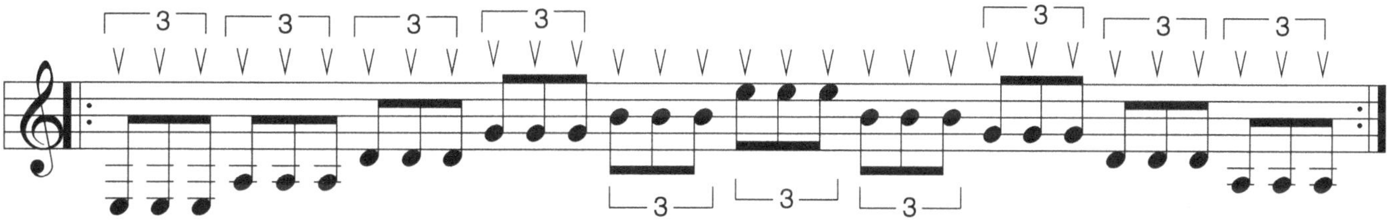

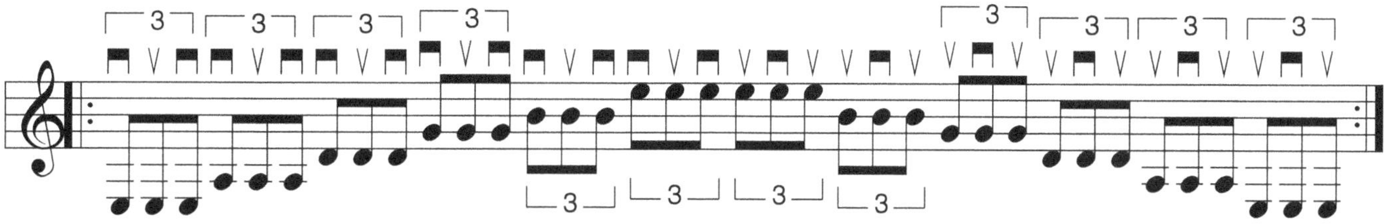

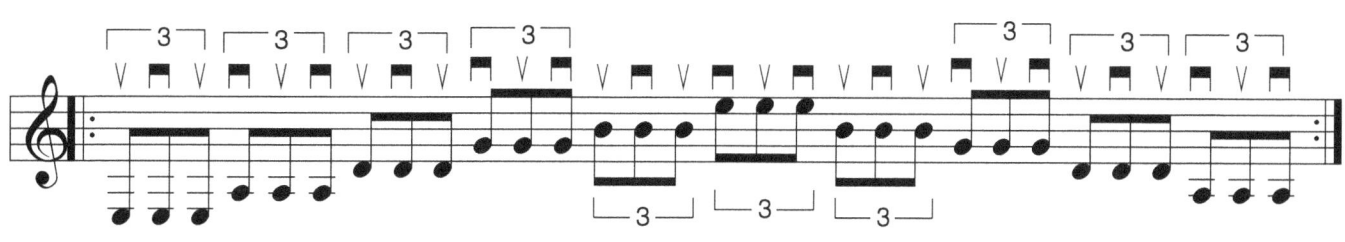

FOUR NOTES PER STRING

Pick each string four times then move to the next string. You can also work on the example 4 and 15 found in the back of this book. Try using both picking patterns with these exercises.

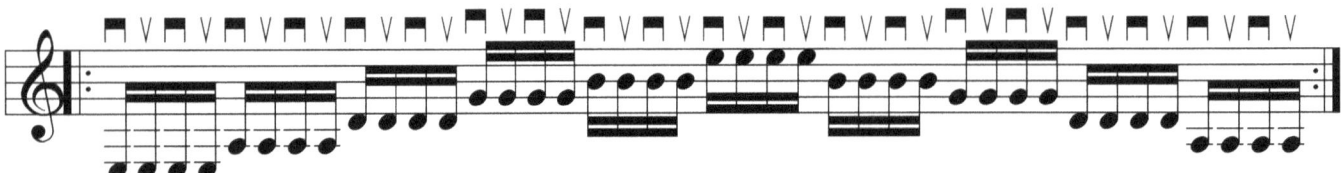

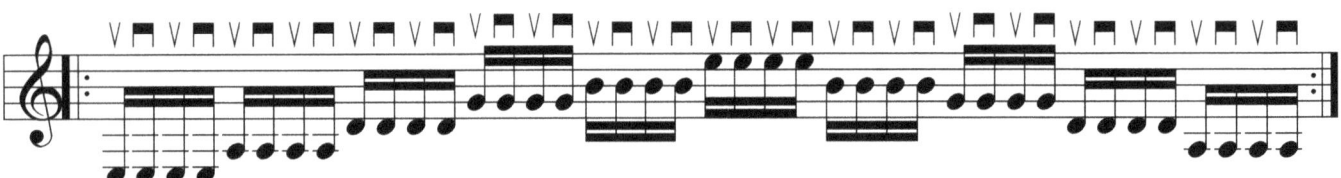

SWEEP AND CROSS STRING PICKING PATTERNS

Some sweep and cross string picking patterns can be played with a combination of elbow movement and forearm movement. The examples found below can be used to develop this technique. I would not attempt this until you feel you have the forearm movement under control. You can also include exercises 5, 6, 7, 8, 9, 11, 12, 17, 18, 19, 20, 23 and 24 found in the back of this book

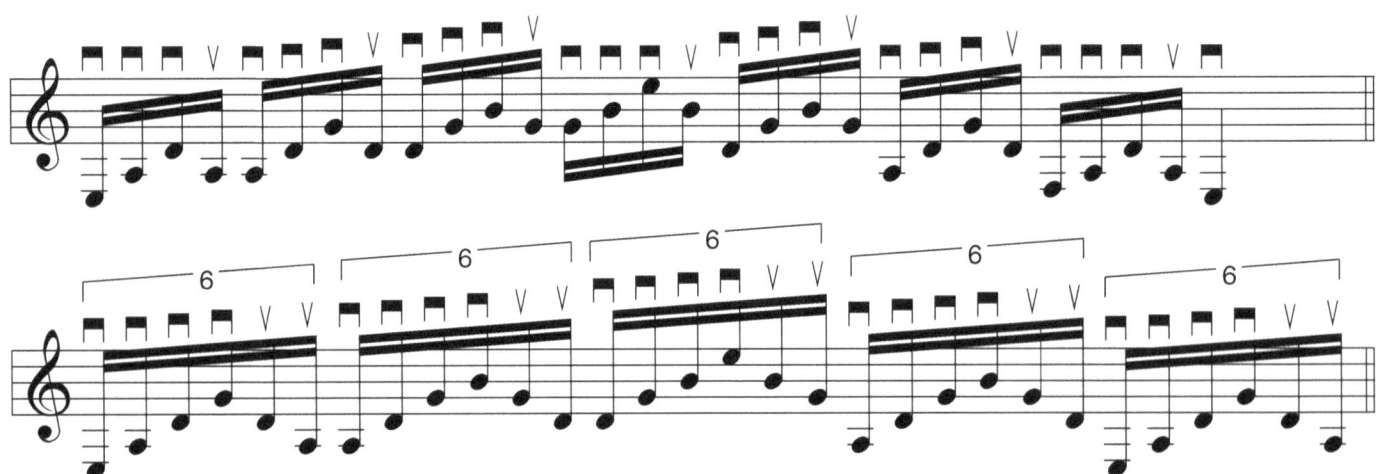

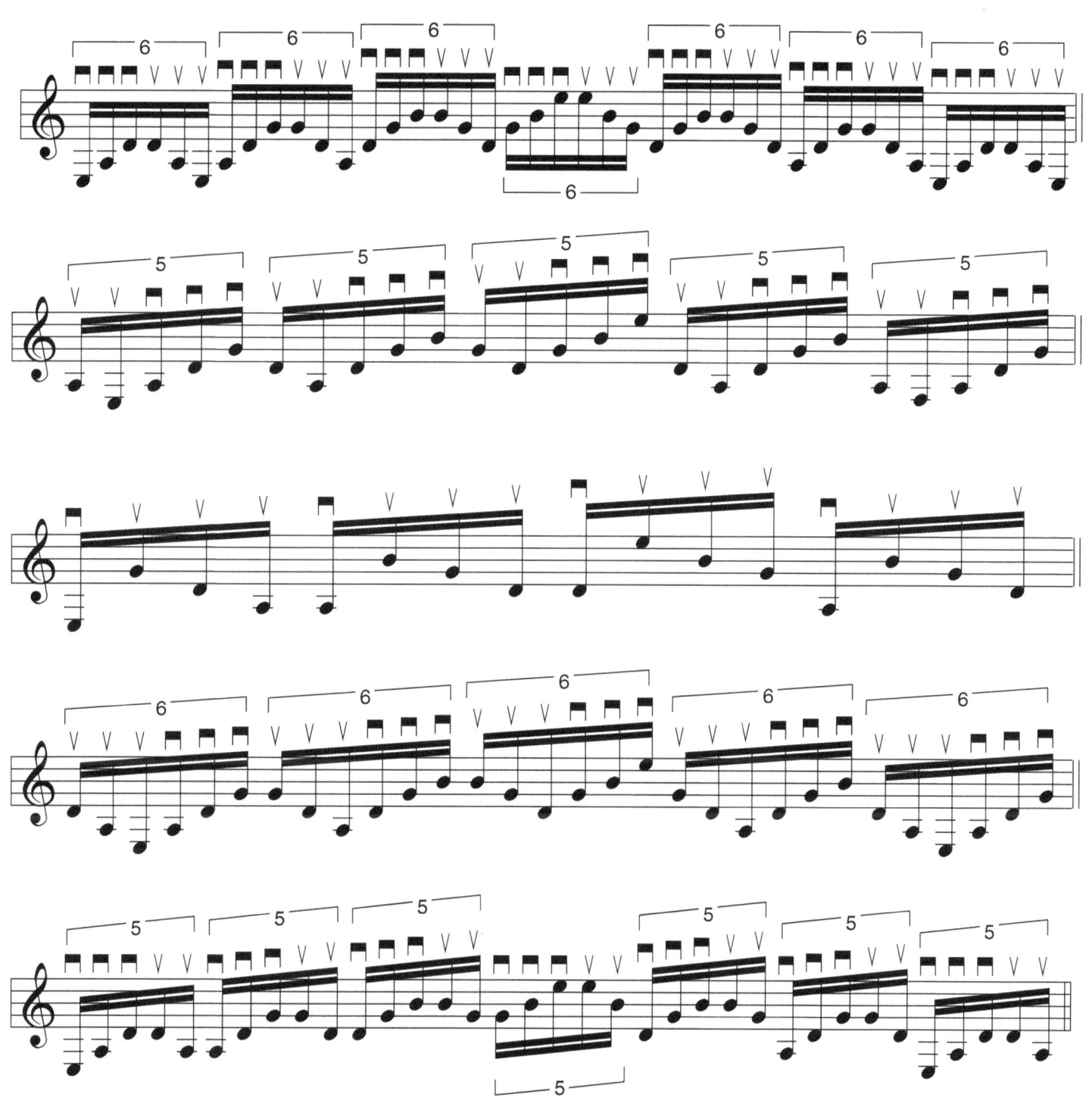

When you are ready you can start to integrate the left hand. I suggest starting with scales or patterns that are familiar to you so that you can still give as much attention to your right hand as possible. See my website at http://www.arnoldjazz.com/workshop for scales studies, sweeps, arpeggios and other techniques to integrate the left hand into your new right hand technique.

EXERCISE 1

EXERCISE 2

EXERCISE 3

EXERCISE 4

31

EXERCISE 5

EXERCISE 6

41

EXERCISE 7

EXERCISE 8

EXERCISE 9

EXERCISE 10

EXERCISE 11

EXERCISE 12

EXERCISE 13

EXERCISE 14

EXERCISE 15

EXERCISE 16

91

EXERCISE 17

EXERCISE 18

EXERCISE 19

EXERCISE 20

EXERCISE 21

EXERCISE 22

EXERCISE 23

EXERCISE 24

Books Available From
Muse Eek Publishing Company

The Bruce Arnold series of instruction books for guitar are the result of 20 years of teaching. Mr. Arnold, who teaches at New York University and Princeton University has listened to the questions and problems of his students, and written forty books addressing the needs of the beginning to advanced student. Written in a direct, friendly and practical manner, each book is structured in such as way as to enable a student to understand, retain and apply musical information. In short, <u>these books teach</u>.

1st Steps for a Beginning Guitarist
Spiral Bound ISBN 1890944-90-4   Perfect Bound ISBN 1890944-93-9

"1st Steps for a Beginning Guitarist" is a comprehensive method for guitar students who have no prior musical training. Whether you are playing acoustic, electric or twelve-string guitar, this book will give you the information you need, and trouble shoot the various pitfalls that can hinder the self-taught musician. Includes pictures, videos and audio in the form of midifiles and mp3's.

Chord Workbook for Guitar Volume 1 (2nd edition)
Spiral Bound ISBN 0-9648632-1-9   Perfect Bound ISBN 1890944-50-5

<u>A consistent seller</u>, this book addresses the needs of the beginning through intermediate student. The beginning student will learn chords on the guitar, and a section is also included to help learn the basics of music theory. Progressions are provided to help the student apply these chords to common sequences. The more advanced student will find the reharmonization section to be an invaluable resource of harmonic choices. Information is given through musical notation as well as tablature.

Chord Workbook for Guitar Volume 2 (2nd edition)
Spiral Bound ISBN 0-9648632-3-5   Perfect Bound ISBN 1890944-51-3

This book is the Rosetta Stone of pop/jazz chords, and is geared to the intermediate to advanced student. These are the chords that any serious student bent on a musical career must know. Unlike other books which simply give examples of isolated chords, this unique book provides a comprehensive series of progressions and chord combinations which are immediately applicable to both composition and performance.

Music Theory Workbook for Guitar Series

The world's most popular instrument, the guitar, is not taught in our public schools. In addition, it is one of the hardest on which to learn the basics of music. As a result, it is frequently difficult for the serious guitarist to get a firm foundation in theory.

Theory Workbook for Guitar Volume 1
Spiral Bound ISBN 0-9648632-4-3   Perfect Bound ISBN 1890944-52-1

This book provides real hands-on application of intervals and chords. A theory section written in concise and easy to understand language prepares the student for all exercises. Worksheets are given that quiz a student about intervals and chord construction using staff notation and guitar tablature. Answers are supplied in the back of the book enabling a student to work without a teacher.

Theory Workbook for Guitar Volume 2
Spiral Bound ISBN 0-9648632-5-1   Perfect Bound ISBN 1890944-53-X

This book provides real hands-on application for 22 different scale types. A theory section written in concise and easy to understand language prepares the student for all exercises. Worksheets are given that quiz a student about scale construction using staff notation and guitar tablature. Answers are supplied in the back of the book enabling a student to work without a teacher. Audio files are also available on the muse-eek.com website to facilitate practice and improvisation with all the scales presented.

Rhythm Book Series

These books are a breakthrough in music instruction, using the internet as a teaching tool! Audio files of all the exercises are easily downloaded from the internet.

Rhythm Primer
Spiral Bound ISBN 0-890944-03-3   Perfect Bound ISBN 1890944-59-9

This 61 page book concentrates on all basic rhythms using four rhythmic levels. All examples use one pitch, allowing the student to focus completely on time and rhythm. All exercises can be downloaded from the internet to facilitate learning. See http://www.muse-eek.com for details

Rhythms Volume 1
Spiral Bound ISBN 0-9648632-7-8   Perfect Bound ISBN 1890944-55-6

This 120 page book concentrates on eighth note rhythms and is a thesaurus of rhythmic patterns. All examples use one pitch, allowing the student to focus completely on time and rhythm. All exercises can be downloaded from the internet to facilitate learning. See http://www.muse-eek.com for details.

Rhythms Volume 2
Spiral Bound ISBN 0-9648632-8-6   Perfect Bound ISBN 1890944-56-4

This volume concentrates on sixteenth note rhythms, and is a 108 page thesaurus of rhythmic patterns. All examples use one pitch, allowing the student to focus completely on time and rhythm. All exercises can be downloaded from the internet to facilitate learning. See http://www.muse-eek.com for details.

Rhythms Volume 3
Spiral Bound ISBN 0-890944-04-1   Perfect Bound ISBN 1890944-57-2

This volume concentrates on thirty second note rhythms, and is a 102 page thesaurus of rhythmic patterns. All examples use one pitch, allowing the student to focus completely on time and rhythm. All exercises can be downloaded from the internet to facilitate learning. See http://www.muse-eek.com for details.

Odd Meters Volume 1
Spiral Bound ISBN 0-9648632-9-4   Perfect Bound ISBN 1890944-58-0

This book applies both eighth and sixteenth note rhythms to odd meter combinations. All examples use one pitch, allowing the student to focus completely on time and rhythm. Exercises can be downloaded from the internet to facilitate learning. This 100 page book is an essential sight reading tool.
See http://www.muse-eek.com for details.

Contemporary Rhythms Volume 1
Spiral Bound ISBN 1-890944-27-0   Perfect Bound ISBN 1890944-84-X

This volume concentrates on eight note rhythms and is a thesaurus of rhythmic patterns. Each exercise uses one pitch which allows the student to focus completely on time and rhythm. Exercises use modern innovations common to twentieth century notation, thereby familiarizing the student with the most sophisticated systems likely to be encountered in the course of a musical career. All exercises can be downloaded from the internet to facilitate learning. See http://www.muse-eek.com for details.

Contemporary Rhythms Volume 2
Spiral Bound ISBN 1-890944-28-9   Perfect Bound ISBN 1890944-85-8

This volume concentrates on sixteenth note rhythms and is a thesaurus of rhythmic patterns. Each exercise uses one pitch which allows the student to focus completely on time and rhythm. Exercise use modern innovations common to twentieth century notation, thereby familiarizing the student with the most sophisticated systems likely to be encountered in the course of a musical career. All exercises can be downloaded from the internet to facilitate learning. See http://www.muse-eek.com for details.

Independence Volume 1
Spiral Bound ISBN 1-890944-00-9   Perfect Bound ISBN 1890944-83-1

This 51 page book is designed for pianists, stick and touchstyle guitarists, percussionists and anyone who wishes to develop the rhythmic independence of their hands. This volume concentrates on quarter, eighth and sixteenth note rhythms and is a thesaurus of rhythmic patterns. The exercises in this book gradually incorporate more and more complex rhythmic patterns making it an excellent tool for both the beginning and the advanced student.

Other Guitar Study Aids

Right Hand Technique for Guitar Volume 1
Spiral Bound ISBN 0-9648632-6-X   Perfect Bound ISBN 1890944-54-8

Here's a breakthrough in music instruction, using the internet as a teaching tool! This book gives a concise method for developing right hand technique on the guitar, one of the most overlooked and under-addressed aspects of learning the instrument. The simplest, most basic movements are used to build fatigue-free technique. Exercises can be downloaded from the internet to facilitate learning. See http://www.muse-eek.com for details.

Single String Studies Volume One
Spiral Bound ISBN 1-890944-01-7   Perfect Bound ISBN 1890944-62-9

This book is an excellent learning tool for both the beginner who has no experience reading music on the guitar, and the advanced student looking to improve their ledger line reading and general knowledge of each string of the guitar. Each exercise concentrates the students attention on one string at a time. This allows a familiarity to form between the written pitch and where it can be found on the guitar along with improving one's "feel" for jumping linearly across the fretboard. Exercises can be downloaded from the internet to facilitate learning. See http://www.muse-eek.com for details.

Single String Studies Volume Two
Spiral Bound ISBN 1-890944-05-X   Perfect Bound ISBN 1890944-64-5

This book is a continuation of Volume One, but using non-diatonic notes. Volume Two helps the intermediate and advanced student improve their ledger line reading and general knowledge of each string of the guitar. Each exercise concentrates the students attention on one string at a time. This allows a familiarity to form between the written pitch and where it can be found on the guitar along with improving one's "feel" for jumping linearly across the fretboard. Exercises can be downloaded from the internet to facilitate learning. See http://www.muse-eek.com for details.

Single String Studies Volume One (Bass Clef)
Spiral Bound ISBN 1-890944-02-5   Perfect Bound ISBN 1890944-63-7

This book is an excellent learning tool for both the beginner who has no experience reading music on the bass guitar, and the advanced student looking to improve their ledger line reading and general knowledge of each string of the bass. Each exercise concentrates a students attention of one string at a time. This allows a familiarity to form between the written pitch and where it can be found on the bass along with improving one's "feel" for jumping linearly across the fretboard. Exercises can be downloaded from the internet to facilitate learning. See http://www.muse-eek.com for details.

Single String Studies Volume Two (Bass Clef)
Spiral Bound ISBN 1-890944-06-8   Perfect Bound ISBN 1890944-65-3

This book is a continuation of Volume One, but using non-diatonic notes. Volume Two helps the intermediate and advanced student improve their ledger line reading and general knowledge of each string of the bass. Each exercise concentrates the students attention on one string at a time. This allows a familiarity to form between the written pitch and where it can be found on the bass along with improving one's "feel" for jumping linearly across the fretboard. Exercises can be downloaded from the internet to facilitate learning. See http://www.muse-eek.com for details.

Guitar Clinic
Spiral Bound ISBN 1-890944-45-9   Perfect Bound ISBN 1890944-86-6

Guitar Clinic" contains techniques and exercises Mr. Arnold uses in the clinics and workshops he teaches around the U.S.. Much of the material in this book is culled from Mr. Arnold's educational series, over thirty books in all. The student wishing to expand on his or her studies will find suggestions within the text as to which of Mr. Arnold's books will best serve their specific needs. Topics covered include: how to read music, sight reading, reading rhythms, music theory, chord and scale construction, modal sequencing, approach notes, reharmonization, bass and chord comping, and hexatonic scales.

Sight Singing and Ear Training Series

The world is full of ear training and sight reading books, so why do we need more?
This sight singing and ear training series uses a different method of teaching relative pitch sight singing and ear training. The success of this method has been remarkable. Along with a new method of ear training these books also use CDs and the internet as a teaching tool! Audio files of all the exercises are easily downloaded from the internet at www.muse-eek.com By combining interactive audio files with a new approach to ear training a student's progress is limited only by their willingness to practice!

A Fanatic's Guide to Ear Training and Sight Singing
Spiral Bound ISBN 1-890944-19-X   Perfect Bound ISBN 1890944-75-0

This book and CD present a method for developing good pitch recognition through sight singing. This method differs from the myriad of other sight singing books in that it develops the ability to identify and name all twelve pitches within a key center. Through this method a student gains the ability to identify sound based on it's relationship to a key and not the relationship of one note to another (i.e. interval training as commonly taught in many texts). All note groupings from one to six notes are presented giving the student a thesaurus of basic note combinations which develops sight singing and note recognition to a level unattainable before this Guide's existence.

Key Note Recognition
Spiral Bound ISBN 1-890944-30-0   Perfect Bound ISBN 1890944-77-7

This book and CD present a method for developing the ability to recognize the function of any note against a key. This method is a must for anyone who wishes to sound one note on an instrument or voice and instantly know what key a song is in. Through this method a student gains the ability to identify a sound based on its relationship to a key and not the relationship of one note to another (i.e. interval training as commonly taught in many texts). Key Center Recognition is a definite requirement before proceeding to two note ear training.

LINES Volume One: Sight Reading and Sight Singing Exercises
Spiral Bound ISBN 1-890944-09-2   Perfect Bound ISBN 1890944-76-9

This book can be used for many applications. It is an excellent source for easy half note melodies that a beginner can use to learn how to read music or for sight singing slightly chromatic lines. An intermediate or advanced student will find exercises for multi-voice reading. These exercises can also be used for multi-voice ear training. The book has the added benefit in that all exercises can be heard by downloading the audio files for each example. See http://www.muse-eek.com for details.

Ear Training ONE NOTE: Beginning Level
Spiral Bound ISBN 1-890944-12-2   Perfect Bound ISBN 1890944-66-1

This is a new method for developing instantaneous recognition of pitches within a key. This contextual-based ear training differs from interval based training by instilling a sense of key relationship; that is, a note is identified by it's characteristic sound within a key, and not by its distance from another note. This method has been used with great success and is now finally available on CD. There are three levels available depending on the student's ability. This beginning level is recommended for students who have little or no music training. A Complete Method book containing the Ear Training One Note Beginning, Intermediate and Advanced levels along with three accompanying CDs is also available for those students wishing to have a complete set of books and CDs under one cover.

Ear Training ONE NOTE: Intermediate Level
Spiral Bound ISBN 1-890944-13-0   Perfect Bound ISBN 1890944-67-X

This is a new method for developing instantaneous recognition of pitches within a key. This contextual-based ear training differs from interval based training by instilling a sense of key relationship; that is, a note is identified by it's characteristic sound within a key, and not by its distance from another note. This method has been used with great success and is now finally available on CD. There are three levels available depending on the student's ability. This intermediate level is recommended for students who have had some music training but still find their skills need more development. A Complete Method book containing the Ear Training One Note Beginning, Intermediate and Advanced levels along with three accompanying CDs is also available for those students wishing to have a complete set of books and CDs under one cover.

Ear Training ONE NOTE: Advanced Level
Spiral Bound ISBN 1-890944-14-9   Perfect Bound ISBN 1890944-68-8

This is a new method for developing instantaneous recognition of pitches within a key. This contextual-based ear training differs from interval based training by instilling a sense of key relationship; that is, a note is identified by it's characteristic sound within a key, and not by its distance from another note. This method has been used with great success and is now finally available on CD. There are three levels available depending on the student's ability. This advanced level is recommended for advanced music students or those who have worked with the intermediate level and now wish to perfect their skills. A Complete Method book containing the Ear Training One Note Beginning, Intermediate and Advanced levels along with three accompanying CDs is also available for those students wishing to have a complete set of books and CDs under one cover.

Ear Training ONE NOTE: Complete Method
Spiral Bound ISBN 1-890944-47-5   Perfect Bound ISBN 1890944-48-3

This is a new method for developing instantaneous recognition of pitches within a key. This contextual-based ear training differs from interval based training by instilling a sense of key relationship; that is, a note is identified by it's characteristic sound within a key, and not by its distance from another note. This Complete Method book contains the Ear Training One Note Beginning, Intermediate and Advanced levels along with three accompanying CDsand is available for those students who wish to have a complete set of books and CDs under one cover.

Ear Training TWO NOTE: Beginning Level Volume One
Spiral Bound ISBN 1-890944-31-9   Perfect Bound ISBN 1890944-69-6

This Book and Audio CD continues the method of developing relative pitch ear training as set forth in the "Ear Training, One Note" series. There are six volumes in the beginning level series. Through practice, the student eventually gains the ability to recognize the key and the names of any two notes played simultaneously. Volume One concentrates on 5ths. Prerequisite: a strong grasp of the One Note method.

Ear Training TWO NOTE: Beginning Level Volume Two
Spiral Bound ISBN 1-890944-32-7   Perfect Bound ISBN 1890944-70-X

This Book and Audio CD continues the method of developing relative pitch ear training as set forth in the "Ear Training, One Note" series. There are six volumes in the beginning level series. Through practice, the student eventually gains the ability to recognize the key and the names of any two notes played simultaneously. Volume Two concentrates on 3rds. Prerequisite: a strong grasp of the One Note method.

Ear Training TWO NOTE: Beginning Level Volume Three
Spiral Bound ISBN 1-890944-33-5   Perfect Bound ISBN 1890944-71-8

This Book and Audio CD continues the method of developing relative pitch ear training as set forth in the "Ear Training, One Note" series. There are six volumes in the beginning level series. Through practice, the student eventually gains the ability to recognize the key and the names of any two notes played simultaneously. Volume Three concentrates on 6ths. Prerequisite: a strong grasp of the One Note method.

Ear Training TWO NOTE: Beginning Level Volume Four
Spiral Bound ISBN 1-890944-34-3   Perfect Bound ISBN 1890944-72-6

This Book and Audio CD continues the method of developing relative pitch ear training as set forth in the "Ear Training, One Note" series. There are six volumes in the beginning level series. Through practice, the student eventually gains the ability to recognize the key and the names of any two notes played simultaneously. Volume Four concentrates on 4ths. Prerequisite: a strong grasp of the One Note method.

Ear Training TWO NOTE: Beginning Level Volume Five
Spiral Bound ISBN 1-890944-35-1   Perfect Bound ISBN 1890944-73-4

This Book and Audio CD continues the method of developing relative pitch ear training as set forth in the "Ear Training, One Note" series. There are six volumes in the beginning level series. Through practice, the student eventually gains the ability to recognize the key and the names of any two notes played simultaneously. Volume Five concentrates on 2nds. Prerequisite: a strong grasp of the One Note method.

Ear Training TWO NOTE: Beginning Level Volume Six
Spiral Bound ISBN 1-890944-36-X   Perfect Bound ISBN 1890944-74-2

This Book and Audio CD continues the method of developing relative pitch ear training as set forth in the "Ear Training, One Note" series. There are six volumes in the beginning level series. Through practice, the student eventually gains the ability to recognize the key and the names of any two notes played simultaneously. Volume Six concentrates on 7ths. Prerequisite: a strong grasp of the One Note method.

Comping Styles Series

This series is built on the progressions found in Chord Workbook Volume One. Each book covers a specific style of music and presents exercises to help a guitarist, bassist or drummer master that style. Audio CDs are also available so a student can play along with each example and really get "into the groove."

Comping Styles for the Guitar Volume Two FUNK
Spiral Bound ISBN 1-890944-07-6   Perfect Bound ISBN 1890944-60-2

This volume teaches a student how to play guitar or piano in a funk style. 36 Progressions are presented: 12 keys of a Major and Minor Blues plus 12 keys of Rhythm Changes A different groove is presented for each exercise giving the student a wide range of funk rhythms to master. An Audio CD is also included so a student can play along with each example and really get "into the groove." The audio CD contains "trio" versions of each exercise with Guitar, Bass and Drums.

Comping Styles for the Bass Volume Two FUNK
Spiral Bound ISBN 1-890944-08-4   Perfect Bound ISBN 1890944-61-0

This volume teaches a student how to play bass in a funk style. 36 Progressions are presented: 12 keys of a Major and Minor Blues plus 12 keys of Rhythm Changes A different groove is presented for each exercise giving the student a wide range of funk rhythms to master. An Audio CD is also included so a student can play along with each example and really get "into the groove." The audio CD contains "trio" versions of each exercise with Guitar, Bass and Drums.

Bass Lines: Learning and Understanding the Jazz-Blues Bass Line
Spiral Bound ISBN 1-890944-94-7   Perfect Bound ISBN 1890944-95-5

This book covers the basics of bass line construction. A theoretical guide to building bass lines is presented along with 36 chord progressions utilizing the twelve keys of a Major and Minor Blues, plus twelve keys of Rhythm Changes. A reharmonization section is also provided which demonstrates how to reharmonize a chord progression on the spot.

Time Series

The Doing Time series presents a method for contacting, developing and relying on your internal time sense: This series is an excellent source for any musician who is serious about developing strong internal sense of time. This is particularly useful in any kind of music where the rhythms and time signatures may be very complex or free, and there is no conductor.

THE BIG METRONOME
Spiral Bound ISBN 1-890944-37-8   Perfect Bound ISBN 1890944-82-3

The Big Metronome is designed to help you develop a better internal sense of time. This is accomplished by requiring you to "feel time" rather than having you rely on the steady click of a metronome. The idea is to slowly wean yourself away from an external device and rely on your internal/natural sense of time. The exercises presented work in conjunction with the three CDs that accompany this book. CD 1 presents the first 13 settings from a traditional metronome 40-66; the second CD contains metronome markings 69-116, and the third CD contains metronome markings 120-208. The first CD gives you a 2 bar count off and a click every measure, the second CD gives you a 2 bar count off and a click every 2 measures, the 3rd CD gives you a 2 bar count off and a click every 4 measures. By presenting all common metronome markings a student can use these 3 CDs as a replacement for a traditional metronome.

Doing Time with the Blues Volume One:
Spiral Bound ISBN 1-890944-17-3   Perfect Bound ISBN 1890944-78-5

The book and CD presents a method for gaining an internal sense of time thereby eliminating dependence on a metronome. The book presents the basic concept for developing good time and also includes exercises that can be practiced with the CD. The CD provides eight 8 minute tracks at different tempos in which the time is delineated every 2 bars, and with an extra hit every 12 bars to outline the blues form. The student may then use the exercises presented in the book to gain control of their execution or improvise to gain control of their ideas using this bare minimum of time delineation.

Doing Time with the Blues Volume Two:
Spiral Bound ISBN 1-890944-18-1   Perfect Bound ISBN 1890944-79-3

This is the 2nd volume of a four volume series which presents a method for developing a musician's internal sense of time, thereby eliminating dependence on a metronome. This 2nd volume presents different exercises which further the development of this time sense. This 2nd volume begins to test even a professional level player's ability. The CD provides eight 8 minute tracks at different tempos in which the time is delineated every 4 bars with an extra hit every 12 bars to outline the blues form. New exercises are also included that can be practiced with the CD. This series is an excellent source for any musician who is serious about developing an internal sense of time.

Doing Time with 32 bars Volume One:
Spiral Bound ISBN 1-890944-22-X   Perfect Bound ISBN 1890944-80-7

The book and CD presents a method for gaining an internal sense of time thereby eliminating dependence on a metronome. The book presents the basic concept for developing good time and also includes exercises that can be practiced with the CD. The CD provides eight 8 minute tracks at different tempos in which the time is delineated every 2 bars, with an extra hit every 32 to outline the 32 bar form. The student may then use the exercises presented in the book to gain control of their execution or improvise to gain control of their ideas using this bare minimum of time delineation.

Doing Time with 32 bars Volume Two:
Spiral Bound ISBN 1-890944-23-8   Perfect Bound ISBN 1890944-81-5

This is the 2nd volume of a four volume series which presents a method for developing a musician's internal sense of time, thereby eliminating dependence on a metronome.. This 2nd volume presents different exercises which further the development of this time sense. This 2nd volume begins to test even a professional level player's ability. The CD provides eight 8 minute tracks at different tempos in which the time is delineated every 4 bars with an extra hit every 32 bars to outline the 32 bar form.   New exercises are also included that can be practiced with the CD. This series is an excellent source for any musician who is serious about developing an internal sense of time.

Other Workbooks

Music Theory Workbook for All Instruments, Volume 1: Interval and Chord Construction
Spiral Bound ISBN 1890944-92-0   Perfect Bound ISBN 1890944-46-7

This book provides real hands-on application of intervals and chords. A theory section written in concise and easy to understand language prepares the student for all exercises. Worksheets are given that quiz a student about intervals and chord construction using staff notation. Answers are supplied in the back of the book enabling a student to work without a teacher.

E-Books

The Bruce Arnold series of instructional E-books is for the student who wishes to target specific areas of study that are of particular interest. Many of these books are excerpted from other larger texts. The excerpted source is listed for each book. These books are available on-line at www.muse-eek.com as well as at many e-tailers throughout the internet. These books can also be purchased in the traditional book binding format. (See the ISBN number for proper format)

Chord Velocity: Volume One, Learning to switch between chords quickly
E-book ISBN 1-890944-88-2   Traditional Book Binding ISBN 1-890944-97-1

The first hurdle a beginning guitarist encounters is difficulty in switching between chords quickly enough to make a chord progression sound like music. This book provides exercises that help a student gradually increase the speed with which they change chords. Special free audio files are also available on the muse-eek.com website to make practice more productive and fun. With a few weeks, remarkable improvement by can be achieved using this method. This book is excerpted from "1st Steps for a Beginning Guitarist Volume One."

Guitar Technique: Volume One, Learning the basics to fast, clean, accurate and fluid performance skills.
E-book ISBN 1-890944-91-2   Traditional Book Binding ISBN 1-890944-99-8

This book is for both the beginning guitarist or the more experienced guitarist who wishes to improve their technique. All aspects of the physical act of playing the guitar are covered, from how to hold a guitar to the specific way each hand is involved in the playing process. Pictures and videos are provided to help clarify each technique. These pictures and videos are either contained in the book or can be downloaded at www.muse-eek.com This book is excerpted from "1st Steps for a Beginning Guitarist Volume One."

Accompaniment: Volume One, Learning to Play Bass and Chords Simultaneously
E-book ISBN 1-890944-87-4   Traditional Book Binding ISBN 1-890944-96-3

The techniques found within this book are an excellent resource for creating and understanding how to play bass and chords simultaneously in a jazz or blues style. Special attention is paid to understanding how this technique is created, thereby enabling the student to recreate this style with other pieces of music. This book is excerpted from the book "Guitar Clinic."

Beginning Rhythm Studies: Volume One, Learning the basics of reading rhythm and playing in time.
E-book ISBN 1-890944-89-0   Traditional Book Binding 1-890944-98-X

This book covers the basics for anyone wishing to understand or improve their rhythmic abilities. Simple language is used to show the student how to read and play rhythm. Exercises are presented which can accelerate the learning process. Audio examples in the form of midifiles are available on the muse-eek.com website to facilitate learning the correct rhythm in time. This book is excerpted from the book "Rhythm Primer."

www.ingramcontent.com/pod-product-compliance
Lightning Source LLC
Chambersburg PA
CBHW080342170426
43194CB00014B/2661